You can recognize *Stegosaurus*
by the large, bony plates—usually 17 of
them—along its back, as well as sharp
spikes on its tail.

Dinosaurs lived during a time called the Mesozoic Era, from about 250 million years ago until about 65 million years ago. This era is made up of three time periods: the Triassic, Jurassic, and Cretaceous.

Tyrannosaurus rex could have up to
60 teeth—that's almost double the
number of teeth that adult humans have.
Each T. rex tooth was around the size
of a banana!

The name *dinosaur* was first used in 1842—many millions of years after dinosaurs lived on Earth—by scientist Richard Owen. The word comes from Greek and is usually translated to "terrible lizard," not because dinosaurs were mean, but because many of them were so big!

Huge plant-eating dinosaurs with long necks and long tails are called sauropods. Among the sauropods were probably some of the largest animals to ever live on our planet.

Scientists who study fossils are called *paleontologists*, and they have found dinosaur fossils on every continent in the world. Paleontologists have identified more than 700 different species (types) of dinosaur.

The head of *Triceratops* is one of the largest of all animals that ever existed. The biggest *Triceratops* had heads that were close to 10 feet (3 meters) long from nose to neck!

Most dinosaurs were *herbivores*,
or plant-eaters, with wide, flat teeth for
chewing leaves and twigs. The *carnivores*,
or meat-eaters, had long, pointy teeth
for chewing tough meat. Dinosaurs
with both types of teeth were probably
omnivores, meaning that they ate
both plants and meat.

Many large dinosaurs had scaly, bumpy skin. Some, including *Ankylosaurus* and *Stegosaurus*, had hard, bony plates or spikes that grew from their skin.

Because dinosaurs lived all over the world, on every continent, their fossils are found in many different types of environments.

Paleobotanists are scientists who study
the fossils of the ancient trees
plants, and flowers that grew in
the areas where dinosaurs lived.

By studying dinosaur skeletons, scientists can figure out how much dinosaurs weighed. The largest ones weighed up to 18 tons—about the same as 12 average-sized cars!

Brachiosaurus is sometimes described as "giraffe-like" because of its long legs and its long neck that stretched high up into the treetops so the dinosaur could eat leaves.

Ankylosaur is a name for the different types of armored dinosaurs. They were protected by thick, hard plates and spikes over most of their bodies and heads, and they often had club-like tails.

You can recognize *Spinosaurus* by the large, bony "sail" on its back. Some scientists believe that *Spinosaurus* was a good swimmer, and its powerful tail helped it move in the water.

To support the heavy "hammer" at its end, the tail of an ankylosaur had to be thick and strong.

Triceratops' name means "three-horned face." It had a horn above each eye and near its nose.

Brontosaurus is the more well-known name of *Apatosaurus*. This dinosaur ate large amounts of plants, and scientists think it may have also eaten rocks to help it digest its food.

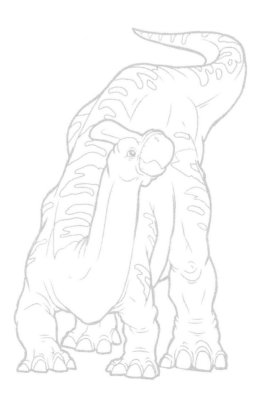

Pterosaur means "winged lizard." These dinosaur relatives had wings made of skin, unlike the feathered wings of birds.

Some dinosaurs lived in swampy areas
where many plants and trees grew,
so the herbivores had a big selection
of things to eat.

Some scientists believe that *herbivorous* (plant-eating) dinosaurs who usually walked on four legs could stand up on their back two legs to reach higher trees and leaves.

Dinosaurs' plates were called *scutes*.
Scutes may have helped a dinosaur keep
its body at a comfortable temperature,
or they may have been just for display.

Researchers have found groups of
fossilized footprints, called *trackways*,
showing that dinosaurs often
traveled together.

Larger pterosaurs could have wingspans of close to 30 feet (more than 9 meters).

Atop a sauropod's very long neck was a tiny head. These dinosaurs didn't need big jaws and strong muscles for chewing, because they did not chew their food!

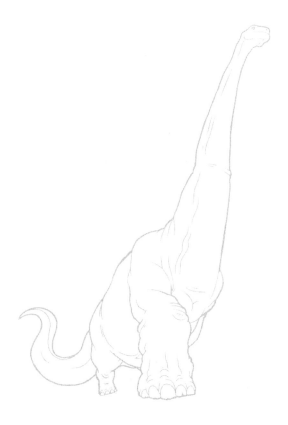

Dinosaurs that walked on two legs and had shorter arms with "hands" often had three curved claws on each hand that they used for grabbing things.

Velociraptors belonged to a group of two-legged dinosaurs called *theropods*. Raptors had feathers but did not fly, and they are some of the earliest relatives of today's birds.

Pachycephalosaurus was known for its large size, its strength, and its domed skull, which was many times thicker than other dinosaurs' skulls.

Although dinosaurs are usually known as being huge creatures, there were many small dinosaurs too—around the size of a turkey or smaller!

Many plant-eating dinosaurs were bigger
than the meat-eaters, and this could be
because it was easier for them to find
and digest large amounts of food.

Pliosaurs were prehistoric reptiles who lived in water. One of the largest was Kronosaurus, which could grow to 40 feet (about 12 meters) long, with a 12-foot (3.7-meter)–long head!

Most dinosaur names come from the Greek language. The word *sauropod* means "lizard foot" in Greek.

Along with its three horns, *Triceratops* has a large, bony frill at the back of its head that makes it easy to recognize.

Dinosaurs who walked on four feet are called *quadrupeds*. Dinosaurs who walked on two feet are called *bipeds*. Some dinosaurs used all four feet to walk but just the back two feet to run.

Carnivorous (meat-eating) dinosaurs had sharp teeth and claws, and even some herbivores (plant-eaters) had sharp claws for grabbing plants and maybe digging for roots.

Dinosaurs with long necks and heavy heads usually also had long tails to help them balance.

T. rex's arms were only about 3 feet
(around 1 meter) long, so they were
tiny compared to the rest of its body.
Scientists do not know for sure how
T. rex used its arms, or if it even
used them at all.

Researchers have learned many things
about dinosaurs, but we will probably
never know what colors dinosaurs were.
Use your imagination!

New discoveries from the 1990s to today show that many dinosaurs, especially those found in China and Russia, had feathers on parts of their bodies. These feathers were probably soft and fluffy, almost like a baby chick's.

Birds are the closest living relatives
to dinosaurs, so it's no surprise to find
out that some dinosaurs had beak-like
structures similar to the beaks of their
modern-day flying cousins.